NORSE

*A Concise Guide to Gods, Heroes, Sagas and Beliefs
of Norse Mythology*

Copyright © 2016 by Hourly History.

Table of Contents

Introduction

If this is indeed your first foray into the subject of Norse mythology, you will find that it calls for an adjustment in the way you see things. You will need to prepare yourself for a very different world, one where there is often no logic as you understand it, no justice as administered by a modern court of law, and very little point in asking "why." It's an amazing world where animals have the power of speech, inanimate objects like swords or hammers have specific names, and where the passage of time is measured by the destruction of the world. It is nevertheless a fascinating, illuminating and richly rewarding world, and your appreciation of where, how, and why you exist will be immeasurably enhanced by what you discover.

Norse mythology covers the pre-Christian history of the countries and peoples of what we now call Scandinavia. The cosmology presents us with a theory of the creation of the world and the first people who dwelt here. These were the guiding beliefs of the people we call the Vikings, who were the adventurers setting off from modern Norway, Sweden, and Denmark and swept through ancient Britain, a nascent Europe, and on into Russia and India in medieval times. Initially appearing and behaving as pillaging raiders from the sea, they built trade routes through the world that are still used to this very day. Their strength and success lay in their skills as shipbuilders and seafarers and their unshakable pagan beliefs in predestination, which dictated that the only honorable way to die was in battle. These were the Norsemen, and one of their descendants is the star of this story.

Snorri Sturluson (1179-1241) was orphaned at an early age and was brought up by Jón Loptsson, possibly the most influential chieftain in Iceland. Snorri married money and settled in Reykjaholt, acquiring a reputation as a scholar, writer, and historian. He was elected twice as the "lawspeaker" in the Iceland High Court. He collected and wrote down as many of the old oral poems on gods and heroes as he could find. He also added his own commentary and extensive writings into what became a kind of poetic handbook which has come down to us as the *Prose Edda*, with "edda" meaning great-grandmother.

One of his sources, a collection of poems by Saemund Sigfusson, was found in 1643 in an old farmhouse in Oddi. This is now known as the *Poetic* (or Elder) *Edda*, and it contains some tales from as early as 800 BCE; riddle contests between the gods and the giants and an amazing version of the creation of the world. Incredibly, these two books are by far the most important and authentic source of Norse mythology that we have, all thanks to the intense interest of one man. There are a few other sources available, but with all being transcriptions of oral history that was recorded hundreds of years after the event and, like the Snorri collection, usually by a Christian.

One of the reasons that the Eddas are such a trustworthy source is that we know from contemporary sources that, although Snorri was Christian, he did not hold the popular opinion that pagan gods were manifestations or personifications of Satan. The Eddas are freely available to be read online as a result of the Project Gutenberg, and you can find them at http://www.gutenberg.org/files/14726/14726-h/14726-h.htm Unless otherwise stated, all quotes used herein come from this specific source. The translations are done from Old Norse by Benjamin Thorpe and I.A. Blackwell. While Snorri sadly came to an untimely end as a result of falling out with the king of Norway, who ordered his assassination, his legacy lives on.

Another paradigm shift we must make before we enter the realm of ancient mythology is the place of the gods in daily life, how real and present they were, and how important. Most people tend to know more about the mythological Greek and Roman pantheons than their Norse counterparts, as they were a much jollier lot. The Greek gods, in particular, lived a pleasurable and joyous life in Olympus—they were immortal, having been created by Mother Earth and Father Heaven. The great Greek heroes were modeled in their likeness and were beautiful, fearless, and performed daring feats with strength and courage.

The Norse gods were more remarkable, not immortal, and constantly at odds with their Giant enemies. They endured great trials and lived in Asgard, which they knew was destined to go up in flames during Ragnarok, or the prophesized end of the world. The Greek gods came before and in fact, created the universe, while in Norse mythology, the universe was created by and from one of the gods. Norse heroes, though similarly enormously strong, were unlike their Greek and Roman counterparts as they were strangely detached, almost solemn, and tended to be tested by performing feats that demanded great sacrifices. Interestingly, in both mythologies, gods and goddesses had equal rights and were just as powerful and forthright.

Chapter One

The Creation in Norse Mythology

"Twas time's first dawn,
When nought yet was,
Nor sand nor sea,
Nor cooling wave;
Earth was not there,
Nor heaven above.
Nought save a void
And yawning gulf.
But verdure none."

The "void and yawning gulf" was called Ginnungagap. To the north was a frozen waste of ice, fog, frost, and bitter cold called Niflheim. In the south was a wasteland called Muspelheim, consumed with fire, smoke, sparks, and oozing lava. These two spheres drifted toward each other through the void, finally colliding; if this sounds vaguely familiar, it is because it echoes the first verses of Genesis in the Bible: "The earth was without form and void, and darkness was over the face of the deep." But then, all familiarity disappears, and in the Eddas we read: "And when the heated blast met the gelid vapour it melted it into drops, and, by the might of him who sent the heat, these drops quickened into life, and took a human semblance. The being thus formed was named Ymir."

Ymir is variously described as the primordial deity or Ice Giant, or a humanoid creature. At the same time and from the same material, the cow Audhumbla was created. Four rivers of milk flowed from her teats which sustained Ymir, who fell asleep after drinking large quantities of her milk. As he slept, two giants, one male and one female, grew from the sweat under Ymir's left armpit. Some versions of the myth say that one giant came from each armpit. Even more startlingly, his legs parted, creating a son called Thrudgelmir or "Strength Yeller." In one version, it was actually a six-headed son that grew out of his feet. However it happened, this was the first of the Frost Giants or the Jotuns.

Audhumbla, the giant cow, sustained herself by licking the salt from the rocks. On the first day, her licking produced an outline of long hair, the second produced a human head, and the third revealed the rest of the body of Buri, the first god. Buri immediately produced a son called Bor or Borr. Bor married a Jotun named Bestla, and they had three mighty sons: Odin, Vili, and Vé.

The Creation of the Earth

It was then, even before the forming of the Earth, that the eternal feud between good and evil began. The *Prose Edda* records it thus:

"'Was there,' asked Gangler, 'any kind of equality or any degree of good understanding between these two races?'
'Far from it,' replied Har; 'for the sons of Bor slew the giant Ymir, and when he fell there ran so much blood from his wounds, that the whole race of Frost-giants was drowned in it, except a single giant, who saved himself with his household.' It is not clear why Ymir was killed and if one visualizes a race of giants drowning in the subsequent bloodshed. One is bound to want to know the reason for

such overwhelming brutality, but as I mentioned above, the one thing we must not do on this journey is ask 'why.'"

The Earth was then created by Bor, Odin, Vili, and Vé out of Ymir's body. From his flesh, they fashioned the Earth. Using his eyebrows and jaw, they built an island stronghold to protect themselves from the Giants and called it Midgard; out of his blood, the seas and lakes were created; out of his bones, the mountains and hills; out of his hair the trees and grasses were fashioned. His skull became the heavens, and his brains were scattered to form the clouds. Worms or maggots crawled out of his skull, and these became the race of dwarves. Four dwarves were chosen to hold up the four corners of the sky: Nordi held up the north, Sundri the south, Austri the east, and Vestri the west. The stars were fashioned from the sparks and burning embers that remained from the tremendous conflagration in Ginnungagap.

The Axis of the Universe

"There stands an ash called Yggdrasil,
A mighty tree showered in white hail.
From there come the dews that fall in the valleys.
It stands evergreen above Urd's Well."

One of the central structures in Norse mythology is the evergreen ash tree called Yggdrasil. There are conflicting versions of how it came to be, but it is regarded as the holiest seat of the gods and where they held council every day. Some say that, like the Earth, it came from Ymir's body while others say it is one with Odin. The Nine Worlds are supported in its branches or enclosed in its three great roots. It draws water from the sacred Well of Urd. This well is pivotal in Norse mythology, and we will return to it time and time again. The waters are so sacred that they run white as an eggshell. This is perhaps the first time that the color white, which encompasses the entire color spectrum, is associated with purity, new beginnings, and awakenings. Two pure white swans—the progenitors of the entire race, are born from this well.

Perched at the top of the tree is an omniscient eagle whose flapping wings provide the great winds that encircle the Earth. Between his eyes sits an eagle called Vedrfolnir. At the bottom of the tree lives Nidhog, a dragon, who gnaws at its roots and keeps company with serpents. The eagle and Nidhog detest each other and spend a great deal of time trading insults via Ratatosk, a gossipy squirrel who runs between the two as a messenger all day. Four stags also live in the branches: Dáinn, Dvalinn, Duneyrr, and Durathror.

This cosmic tree is maintained by three women who appear in similar guises in Greek, Roman, and Norse mythology and are very important to both gods and humans: they are the Fates who determine destiny. In the Greek and Roman pantheon, they represent the "thread of life," the "length of the thread," and the "cutter of the thread." In Norse mythology, they are Urder, she who knows the past, Verdandi, she who controls the present, and Skuld, the youngest, who prepares the future. They water the roots of the tree every day from the Well of Urd, and, each morning, they put a very noisy rooster at the top of the tree. They don't tolerate much back-chat either.

The Creation of Humans

One day, Bor's sons were strolling along the beach and they found two logs—one from an ash tree and one from an elm tree. From each log they fashioned a human being, one male and one female. Odin gave them life and a lively spirit, Vili gifted them shape, speech, feelings, and five senses, and Vé endowed them with movement, mind, and intelligence. The man was named Ask, and the woman was named Embla. "From these two descend the whole human race whose assigned dwelling was within Midgard."

A man called Mundilfari quickly caused the gods some chagrin. He had two children who were breathtakingly lovely to look on. He named his gentle and graceful daughter Sol (sun) and the striking and handsome son Mani (moon). The gods, finding this very presumptuous, placed the children in the heavens. Sol was commanded to drive the horses Arvak (Early Rising) and Alsvid (Very Fast) who pulled the chariot of the sun, which the gods had made to give light to the Earth, across the sky. Her brother Mani was told to guide the passage of the moon and control its waxing and waning.

Odin, also known as the All-father, used the same kind of strategy to form the night and the day—but this time he turned to the Jotuns instead: "Then took All-father, [Nott] Night, and [Dagr] Day, her son, and gave them two horses and two chariots, and set them up in the heavens that they might drive successively one after the other, each in twelve hours' time, round the world." The first to ride out is Night, on her horse called Hrimfaxi. The night ride is long, and as Hrimfaxi comes to the end of the journey, his coat is gleaming and covered in foam. As he shakes his bridle, the foam covers the earth and humans see it as light dew as the day breaks. Skinfaxi is the name of Day's horse; his mane is so luxurious and full that it sheds light over heaven and earth.

Chapter Two

The Nine Worlds of Norse Mythology

Three of the Nine Worlds are above the Earth. The first of these is the headquarters of the Æsir gods: **Asgard**, sometimes referred to as Asgarör. It has 540 halls, one of which belongs to Odin. Odin's hall is called Valaskjalf, and it stands out even among the other great dwellings because of its pure silver roof. Some sources say that the entire building was made of silver. The throne is called Hlidskjalf, and when Odin sits in it, he can see over the entire world. On the far side is a rainbow bridge, called Bifrost, which allows the gods passage to the world of men. "The gods made a bridge from earth to heaven, and called it Bifrost. Thou must surely have seen it; but, perhaps, thou callest it the rainbow." Dead heroes will pass through Asgard on their way to dwell in Valhalla. Thrudheim, the Place of Might, is also located here and this is where you will find Thor when he is not busy.

Muspelheim, or Muspell, is the second of these worlds considered to be above the Earth. This is the land of primordial fire, ruled by the evil fire giant Surt (Black) who guards the entrance with a blazing sword. Surt has burning hair and is covered in glowing lava, and has little to do in Norse mythology until the end of the world, when he plays a pivotal role. Essentially, Muspelheim is a no-man's land, though some sources say that the fire giants and fire demons dwell here. "Muspell is a world too luminous and glowing to be entered by those who are not indigenous there."

The third world set above the Earth is **Alfheimr**, the home of the Light Elves. These are the beautiful and youthful minor gods of nature and fertility considered to bring inspiration in the spheres of art and music and ruled by the major god Freyr. Sometimes mocked and described as puny because of their lightness and luminosity, they can easily punch above their weight as they are highly skilled in the art of magic.

The main world located on the Earth is **Midgard**, sometimes called Mannheim, or the world of humans. The entire world is encircled by an evil serpent, Jormungand, who stabilises his hold by biting his own tail. Bifrost, the rainbow bridge, ends in Midgard.

The second Earth-bound world is Vanaheim, or **Vanaheimr**, and it is also the home of the Vanir, who are gods but a particular group separate from the Æsir. These Vanir are particularly associated with fertility, wisdom, and the ability to see into the future.

Trouble started between the gods when the Vanir goddess Freya visited Asgard. Freya practiced a powerful kind of witchcraft which could manipulate one's destiny. The Æsir found this very seductive and often used her services. Eventually, they began to realize that they were being led astray from their basic beliefs by their greedy desires. However, instead of looking at themselves for the fault, they turned on her Freya instead, calling her Gullveig, or "greedy for gold." The Æsir attempted to kill Freya, but she rose from her ashes three times. Unwisely, the Æsir decided to go to war with the Vanir, even after such a display of immortality. "Broken was the outer wall of the Æsir's burgh. The Vanir, foreseeing conflict, tramp o'er the plains. Odin cast [his spear], and mid the people hurled it: that was the first warfare in the world."

Neither side could gain the upper hand for long, and fairly soon the divinities became weary and bored by the fighting. As such, a truce was declared. To establish and cement good faith, each side sent several "hostages" to live with the other tribe. Freya, Freyr, and Njord went to live in Asgard, and Hoenir and Mimer moved to Vanaheimr. This truce has been honored, and, although their spheres of expertise are different, they often overlap with no friction; both tribes or races have important roles to play. For instance, the guardian of the vital Bifrost bridge is the Vanir god, Heimdall.

The last earth-bound world is that of **Jutonheim**. This is the realm of the Jotuns or Giants, also known as Etins. It is a cold place; flat around the edges and rocky and mountainous with overgrown wild forests toward the interior. There are Frost or Rime Giants, Ice Giants, Mountain Giants, and Storm Giants. They are between 20 to 30 feet tall; strong with flesh and bone density three times that of humans. They are vulnerable to heat and function best in their own environment. The Giant god Mimir's Well of Wisdom is placed here, where he guards it. Often referred to as the god of prophecy, Mimir remained so still that he became part of a great mountain surrounding the well.

The Jotun are constantly at loggerheads with the Æsir. They are led by Utgard-Loki, the Æsir god of mischief; despite implacable dislike between the Frost Giants and the Æsir, there is much intermarriage between two. Loki himself is the son of the Giant king Lunvey. Additionally, the Jotun were technically there first—the very first deity that was created was Ymir, after all.

This brings us to the three underground worlds said to be among the roots of the Cosmic Tree—things get a bit murky here, as not all sources agree with one another. Firstly, there is **Svartalfheim**, the world of the Dark Elves. These creatures hate the light and the sun and will turn to stone if exposed to either. They annoy and threaten humans a great deal, mainly via nightmares or by haunting animals. This may also be where the dwarves reside as well, but that is not clear.

Next is **Nidavellir**. This is where most sources put the realm of the dwarves. The dwarves play a vital part in Norse mythology mainly because they are such excellent craftsmen. In addition to being the most gifted at craftwork, they are also masters of magic and sorcery. They are constantly being called upon by the gods to create important and ingenious artifacts for all kinds of occasions, typically being requested to craft crowns, jewelry, fetters, magic containers, weapons, vases, and so on.

Many of the myths depend on the result of their skills, such as when Odin was at his wits end on how to bind the ferocious wolf Fenrir. Odin sent a messenger into Nidavellir looking for a craftsman skilled enough to finally create something that would restrain Fenrir. It was obvious that whatever it was needed to be backed up by some kind of sorcery to render it fail-safe, and dwarves were up for the challenge. They forged a restraint called Gleipnir. "It was fashioned out of six things; to wit, the noise made by the footfall of a cat; the beards of women; the roots of stones; the sinews of bears; the breath of fish; and the spittle of birds." When applied, it was the first restraint to work. This quote from the Eddas demonstrates the confusion as to where the dwarves reside.

Finally, there is **Niflheim**—the place of the mists and the coldest and most inhospitable world. Here is located the well of Hvergelmir which means "bubbling" or "boiling spring." Hvergelmir is guarded by the dragon Nidhug and it is the point from which all living proceeded and to which all living will return. The Eddas say that there is a gate in this world that opens into "the abode of death." This refers to the fact that, deep inside Niflheim is Helheim, the realm of the dead. It is ruled by the goddess Hel or Hela, and it is the home of those who do not die in battle. Unlike the Christian hell, it is icy and cold.

Chapter Three

The Major Gods and Goddesses

When one is exploring the world of the gods and goddesses, it is as well to remember that several of them go by different names at different times. They are also very good at assuming names for short periods, particularly when they are on a mission of some sort, more often than not because they are up to some sort of mischief. When, for instance, Freya visited Asgard, precipitating the Æsir-Vanir war, she went in disguise as Heiðr or "Bright," a sorcerer. An excellent online source of brief biographies for the many gods and goddesses you will come across at: http://www.sunnyway.com/runes/gods2.html, but here are some of the most important characters.

Odin is the main and key god in Norse mythology. Not to put too fine a point on it, he said: "I call myself Grim and Ganglari, Herian, Hialmberi, Thekk, Third, Thunn, Unn, Helblindi, High, Sann, Svipal, Sanngetal, Herteit, Hnikar, Bileyg, Baleyg, Bolverk, Fiolnir, Grimnir, Glapsvinn, Fiolsvinn, Sidhott, Sidskegg, Sigfather, Hnikud, All-father, Atrid, Farmatyr, Oski ("God of Wishes"), Omi, Just-as-high, Blindi, Gondlir, Harbard, Svidur, Svidrir, Ialk, Kialar, Vidur, Thror, Ygg, Thund, Vakr, Skilfing, Vafud, Hropta-Tyr, Gaut, Veratyr." He is the god of war and battle but also of thought, logic, and poetry. He is often referred to as All-father. Described as a large man when outside the confines of his hall, Odin is depicted with a cloak, a staff, and a large brimmed hat. This hat is pulled down low to disguise the fact that he only has one eye, as he sacrificed the other at the Well of Urd to gain inner wisdom which he prizes above all things. When riding into battle, you see him on his amazing eight-legged steed Sleipnir, with the ever-present ravens on his shoulders: Huginn (Thought) and Muninn (Memory). He is also accompanied by two wolves: Geri (Greedy) and Freki (Ravenous). He married three times, to Fjorgyn, Frigga, and Rind. His sons were Thor, Balder, Hoder, Tyr, Bragi, Heimdall, Uil, Hermod, Vidar, and Vali. The latter two were destined to survive Ragnarok.

As part of his quest for wisdom, Odin wanted to learn the knowledge and power of runes. For this, he had to wound himself with his own sword, Gungnir, and then hang on Yggdrasil with a noose around his neck for nine days and nights. Each night he would learn a new secret.

> *"I know that I hung,*
> *on a wind-rocked tree,*
> *nine whole nights,*
> *with a spear wounded,*
> *and to Odin offered,*
> *myself to myself;*
> *on that tree, of which no one knows*
> *from what root it springs.*
> *Bread no one gave me,*
> *nor a horn of drink,*
> *downward I peered,*
> *to runes applied myself,*
> *wailing learnt them,*
> *then fell down thence."*

The tale of Sleipnir, Odin's horse, bears retelling as well. Just after the war between the Vanir and the Æsir, one of the Giants offered to build an impenetrable wall around

Asgard over the course of three seasons to provide permanent protection to the Æsir. The price he proposed was very high—he wanted the Sun, the Moon, and the goddess Freya's hand in marriage. The jittery gods wanted the sturdy wall built and, with the proviso that the Giant had to perform the task on his own with the help of just one horse, they agreed, as the Æsir felt it was an impossible task.

The Giant's horse, Svadilfari, was so strong and tireless that he could just as well have been an army helping to build the wall. The gods panicked when they saw that the Giant might meet the deadline, so they sent Loki to put a spanner in the works. Loki transformed himself into a mare in heat and led Svadilfari astray, which prevented the Giant from completing the task. However, Loki found himself with foal; thus was Sleipnir born and gifted to Odin. Inheriting great strength and stamina, Sleipnir was also courageous, noble and extremely fast. He had eight legs, one for each dimension and direction in heaven, and he was the only steed who could carry his rider to the Land of the Dead and back. His name meant "Gliding," and there is an interesting link to the Vikings in this myth.

In about 900 CE, the Vikings imported horses to Iceland from Norway. These horses had two extra gaits as well as the normal walk, trot and canter. One was called the Tölt or "running walk" and the other the Flying Pace. This is a two-beat lateral gait and is now used for competitions. An Icelandic horse in action actually looks as if it could have eight legs as it glides by. "Loki ... bore a grey foal with eight legs. This is the horse Sleipnir, which excels all horses ever possessed by gods or men." The great god Odin and his faithful horse Sleipnir came to be inseparable.

Thor was Odin's son, and he is somewhat more spectacular in appearance. The god of thunder and lightning, also of the sky, fertility, and law and order, Thor had a bushy, red beard, a huge appetite, and a quick temper, though his bouts of anger would be here and gone in a flash. He is always depicted with three items in his possession: a magic belt, Megingjard, which doubles his strength; his hammer, called Mjölnir; and the iron gloves he needed to wield the weapon.

The mighty iron hammer was forged for him by two dwarves, Sindri and Brokkr, though it is variously depicted as a mallet and sometimes an axe as well as a hammer. It could change size, even fitting inside his tunic if need be, and it always returned to his hand. His chariot was drawn by two goats, Tanngrisnir, meaning "gap-toothed," and Tanngnjóstr, meaning "tooth-grinder." Their journeys created thunder, and lightning flashed from a whetstone embedded in Thor's skull. His hall is called Bilskirnir. He married the goddess Sif—though he kept the goddess Jarnsaxa as his mistress as well. He had two daughters called Magni and Modi and a son called Thrud.

One day the Giant king Thrym stole Thor's hammer and demanded the goddess Freya should become his wife in exchange for its return. The gods were not amused and, as they often did, they called upon Loki to devise a plan to get them out of this fix. The gods pretended to acquiesce to the ransom demand, and the day of the marriage was set; their plan involved Thor taking Freya's place at the altar. Thor, as you can imagine, was not much impressed with the scheme. "Then said Thor, the mighty As: 'Me the Æsir will call womanish, if I let myself be clad in bridal raiment.'" The god Loki, not one to mince words, pointed out that Thor's hammer in the hands of the Jotuns could only lead to an unacceptable loss of defensive capabilities to the Æsir and might put the entire Asgard at risk.

So, a grumpy Thor dressed as a splendid bride and Loki made a convincing bridesmaid. At the wedding feast, Thor was in such a bad mood that he ate all the food and drink that had been prepared for the guests. Loki explained that the bride had been so excited prior to the wedding that she had not eaten nor drunk for eight days and that was why she was so very famished. Entranced by this, Thrym peeped under his bride-to-be's veil and was startled by the fierce and fiery eyes that met his gaze. Loki hastened to say that she was feverish with desire for the marriage bed, and that did it for Thrym. He called for the hammer to be brought from its hiding place, eight fathoms under the Earth, so that he could swear his marriage vows on it. Mjölnir was laid on the bride's lap. "Then said Thrym: 'Bring the hammer in, the bride to consecrate; lay Miollnir on the maiden's knee; unite us each with other by the hand of Vor.' Laughed [Thor's] soul in his breast, when the fierce-hearted his hammer recognized." Thor ripped off his veil and killed all the giants that were at the feast. This is how Thor and Mjölnir were re-united.

Baldur, the Bright One, was another of Odin's sons, one from his marriage to Frigga, and a very different person compared to Thor. He was the god of light, love, reconciliation, and radiance, and was very beautiful to behold. He was married to Nanna, the goddess of joy.

It was said that sacred wells sprang up from the hoof marks of Baldur's horse. He was goodness and kindness personified, and perhaps a bit of a momma's boy. However, Frigga experienced disturbing dreams about something terrible happening to Baldur. She then went all around the worlds and made every plant and creature she could find promise not to do anything to harm him. Everyone agreed—everyone, that is, but the Mistletoe, to which Frigga did not speak. It soon became known that, because of Frigga's agreements, Baldur was now impervious to injury and a silly party trick developed where guests would throw all kinds of odd missiles at him during banquets and laugh as they bounced off him.

Loki, the prankster and devious one, made a lethal dart of mistletoe which he took to the next big banquet. He didn't have to wait too long until the game started. Loki sidled up to the blind god Hoder and asked, in an undertone, why he was not joining in the fun. Hoder pointed out that apart from the fact that he had nothing suitable to throw he was not able to see where Baldur was standing. "'Come then,' said Loki, 'do like the rest, and show honour to Baldur by throwing this twig at him, and I will direct thy arm, toward the place where he stands.'" The trusting Hoder then threw the mistletoe dart. Aided by his excellent hearing and the wily Loki, Hoder hit the mark, and Baldur was "pierced through and through, [and] fell down lifeless." The gods were stunned at this turn of events and during the uproar as a consequence of this atrocious deed, Loki slipped away and went on the run.

Loki is surely the most puzzling of the Norse gods. He was neither an Æsir nor a Vanir but was of the race of elementals called Etins and was originally their god of fire. He was actually the son of a Giant, but he tricked his way into becoming Odin's blood brother. He was known as a shapeshifter, a trickster, the Sky Traveler, and the Father-of-Lies. He married Glut (Glow), who bore him two daughters, Eisa (Embers) and Einmyria (Ashes). He also coupled with the giantess Angrboda and produced three monsters: Hel, the goddess of the dead; Jormungand, the great serpent who encircles Midgard; and Fenrir, or Fenris the Wolf. With his third wife, Sigyn, he had two children, Vali and Narfi, who would later have a hand in his capture.

Loki was good-looking, charming, ingenious, and amoral; his pranks often had a twist of viciousness. On the other hand, the gods often called on him to get them out of tight spots. The killing of Baldur was, however, a prank that had gone too far, and the Æsir set about to capture him. After many evasions, they eventually trapped him in a cave. Vali and Narfi, Loki's children, were also captured, and the gods turned Vali into a wolf who attacked and tore his brother, Narfi, apart. Narfi's entrails were used to bind Loki to three flat, heavy stones: one around his chest, one around his loins, and one around his knees—these entrails then turned into iron.

Skadi, the goddess of wintertime havoc who leads the Wild Hunt and who holds wolves and venomous snakes sacred, and the one after whom Scandinavia is named, then fastened such a snake over Loki's head so that it would drip venom onto his face. Sigyn was allowed to sit with him, holding a bowl over Loki's head, to collect the venom. Unfortunately, when she had to leave him to empty the bowl, the venom dripped into his eyes. This caused Loki to shudder violently, triggering an earthquake so severe that it tormented mankind: "But while she [Sigyn] is doing this, venom falls upon Loki, which makes him howl with horror, and twist his body about so violently that the whole earth shakes, and this produces what men call earthquakes." Nevertheless, Loki was destined to lie there in chains until Ragnarok.

Freya is the most beautiful Norse goddess. She presides over love, fertility, lust, war, battle, wealth, and death, so it will not surprise you to know that she also leads the Valkyries. The cat is her sacred animal, and her chariot is drawn by two cats, though sometimes she is shown riding a boar. She was initially married to a mysterious god called Od who suddenly left her and subsequently disappeared. This caused her to shed tears of red gold. She practiced a form of Norse magic called seiðr, and she had a special magic cloak of falcon feathers which allowed her to turn into a bird.

Freya is usually depicted wearing an exquisite necklace called Brisingamen. This was wrought for her by four dwarves. The price she paid was to spend one night with each dwarf. Loki (who else?) ran to Odin with this scandal, and the All-father ordered Loki to steal the necklace from her. This was a lot easier said than done, as getting into Freya's well-guarded hall, Sessrumnir, was difficult and called for much shape shifting on Loki's part. First, he had to turn himself into a fly to get through a crack in the fortress and then, finding her asleep wearing the necklace, with her chin concealing the clasp, he had to turn into a flea and bite her on the opposite cheek. As she turned her head in her sleep, Loki was able to unclasp Brisingamen and flee in his own guise. Odin refused to return the necklace to Freya until she had stirred up war among human beings.

One of the less attractive things about Odin, who was Freya's lover, was that he spent a great deal of his time stirring up war and discontent. This was to produce as many heroic warriors as possible to fight on the gods' side at Ragnarok. Freya, with the other Valkyries, watched over all wars and battles. They selected the fighters who would live and die.

Freyr was Freya's twin brother, and he was the horned god of fertility—also the god of sun, rain, harvests, and prosperity as well as the protector of ships. He rides a golden boar called Gullenbarsti, and he commands a magical ship, Skidbladnir, which always sails in the right direction, can never sink, and can change shape and size to fit in his pocket. Freyr is the ruler of the Light Elves in Alfheimr, who were the ones that built his ship Skidbladnir with a combination of skill, ingenuity, and sorcery. She was large enough to accommodate all the Æsir with their weapons and war stores and equipped with the equivalent of an Elven Norse GPS so that she never became lost at sea.

These features are described by Snorri Sturluson in the Eddas: "As soon as the sails are set a favourable breeze arises and carries her to her place of destination, and she is made of so many pieces, and with so much skill, that when she is not wanted for a voyage Frey may fold her together like a piece of cloth, and put her in his pocket." Skidbladnir had one other fabulous attribute: she could sail on the sea, in the air, and over land.

Freyr is said to be an ancestor of the Yngling family who once ruled what is now Scandinavia.

Chapter Four

Valhalla

*"Five hundred doors
And forty more
Methinks are in Valhalla.
Eight hundred heroes through each door
Shall issue forth
Against the wolf to combat."*

*"A wolf hangs before the western door,
over it an eagle hovers."*

It is now time to talk about Valhalla, the Hall of the Battle Slain. This was the mythical place that inspired the most intrepid adventurers of the past, the Vikings, to hurl themselves into the most perilous journeys in uncharted waters and land on unknown shores, armed only with their swords, armor made of boar skin, and their lust for life. Each warrior believed that the only proper way to die was in doing heroic deeds in battle. Those who fell would be swept up and carried on horseback by the Valkyrie, either to Valhalla to dwell with Odin, or to Fólkvangr to dwell with Freya.

There is some dissension about the exact location of Valhalla. Most sources place it in Asgard, but there is a body of evidence that indicates that it might be elsewhere, perhaps even in Helheim. However, all agree on what happens there. Odin certainly presides there, and the heroes' wounds are healed; they live there forevermore, improving on their battle skills, feasting on meat and mead until the call to the great battle of Ragnarok—the end of the world. These heroes were known as Einherjar.

Chapter Five

Ragnarok

Ragnarok is the predestined end of the cycle of Norse mythology. It is for this great and final battle, which they know they will lose, that all the warrior gods, aided by the valiant human and mythical heroes from Valhalla, have lived and died and will die again. There will be signs which oddly enough will first manifest in Midgard. Human bonds of kinship as well as traditional beliefs will shrivel and disappear. A listless anarchy will evolve. Then there will be a period of time known as Fimbulvetr, characterized by three winters of increasing severity with no summers in between. Three roosters will crow: the crimson rooster Fjalar will crow to the Giants; the golden cock Gullinkambi will crow to the gods; and a third cock will raise the dead. The sun will be devoured by the wolf, Skoll, while his brother, Hati, will eat the moon, leaving the world in darkness. Earthquakes will set Fenrir the Great Wolf free, and he will open his mouth so wide that his upper jaw captures heaven and his lower jaw the Earth, and he will rampage through all the Nine Worlds, destroying all that lives. Great mountains will fall in on their foundations. The seas will overrun the land as the serpent Jormungand comes ashore.

"On the waters floats the ship Naglfar, which is constructed of the nails of dead men. For which reason great care should be taken to die with pared nails, for he who dies with his nails unpared, supplies materials for the building of this vessel, which both gods and men wish may be finished as late as possible. But in this flood shall Naglfar float, and the giant Hrym be its steersman". A second ship from Hel will set sail with Loki at the helm, and the Fire Giants, led by the god Surt, will head for the battlefield, scorching the Earth as they march.

Then, the one who guards Bifrost, the beautiful Heimdall, will sound his horn. Odin, All-father, will rally his warriors and head for the battle plain of Vigrid. First, Odin will ride to Mimir's Well to consult other gods on a suitable battle plan. Yggdrasil, the great Cosmic Tree, will start to shake, and that will bring fear into every heart, even the most brave, as this will signal that Ragnarok is upon them. "The Æsir and all the heroes of Valhalla arm themselves and speed forth to the field, led on by Odin, with his golden helm and resplendent cuirass, and his spear called Gungnir."

Ferocious hand-to-hand battle will take place: Thor will defeat the serpent; Baldur will be killed by Loki; Heimdall will kill Loki; Surt will defeat Freyr. Odin dies fighting Fenrir, who swallows him whole. "After this, Surtur darts fire and flame over the Earth, and the whole universe is consumed." It then sinks into the sea, creating another Ginnungagap. This initiates another cycle of the myth, and it is this cyclical nature of the story which makes it so very different from the Christian version of the creation which has a very linear structure.

Chapter Six

The Sagas

The word saga comes from Old Norse and means "that which is told." It is entirely an oral tradition. While the most common definition of a saga is a medieval, Icelandic, or Norse prose narrative of achievements and events in the history of a person or family, a second definition broadens the scope to what is more widely accepted today: Norse or Scandinavian mythology. This is the history of North Germanic people, stemming from Norse paganism and continuing after the Christianization of Scandinavia and into the folklore of modern time.

Originally, the sagas were retold by the elders of the community or the professional Skalds as they traveled around the country. The setting for these tales to be told could be the warm, family longhouse on a bitterly cold, long winter night or the splendiferous banquet hall of a great king. This storytelling was taken very seriously as it commemorated and extended the history of the various tribes and instilled the necessary faith and proper goals among the young.

Being a skilled poet and Skald was a big deal as can be demonstrated in the life of Egill Skallagrimsson, a poet, warrior, and slaughterer of many men as well as an Icelandic farmer. His frank tales and sagas put him on the wrong side of Erik Blood-Axe, at times king of Norway, who eventually grew impatient with his crimes and endless impudence, arrested him, and sentenced him to death in the morning. Egill spent the night composing an epic poem called the Höfudlausn (Head-Ransom). He was allowed to recite the poem the next morning before his execution, and the Blood-Axe was so moved by the power and the beauty of the poem that he forgave Egill for all his wrongdoing. Here is a brief extract:

"The scream of swords,
The clash of shields,
These are true words
On battlefields:
Man sees his death
Frozen in dreams,
But Eirik's breath
Frees battle-streams.
The war-lord weaves
His web of fear,
Each man receives
His fated share:
A blood-red sun's
The warrior's shield,
The eagle scans
The battlefield.
As edges swing,
Blades cut men down.
Eirik the King
Earns his renown."

This is a translation of the poem by Hermann Palsson and Paul Edwards for *Penguin*. You can read the entire poem online at: http://www.odins-gift.com/pclass/hoefudlausn.htm

This legend might seem farfetched, especially when you look at the elemental and conflict-prone lives of the people of the time. However, the gift of poetry was highly regarded; the rules of composition were extremely taxing, and the play on words and ingenuity of plot a matter for serious consideration. It is not an exaggeration to say that verbal battles could be as treacherous and dangerous as a battle on the field and the rewards and losses similarly consequential.

The sagas dealt with fate, luck, honor, the supernatural, and prophecy. Always in the background was the eternal quandary of good against evil. The Norse people believed in predestination and did not feel it was important to explain people's actions as "each must do as destiny decides." Life was full of epic blood feuds. The themes taught the importance of protecting the household and homestead, competition with outsiders, and the danger of treachery and trickery. The sagas were filled with doom and gloom but "laced with gleams of grandeur and sparks of humor."

Tales of heroism abounded, and the heroes and gods were required to accept their fate and destiny with reckless disregard. The traits of the heroic warrior were courage, honor, and generosity. Society in medieval Iceland made little distinction between the sexes, particularly in their storytelling. People were not divided by their gender but by how physically able and skilled they were. The tales were full of powerful matriarchs, faithful and faithless wives, and trouble-stirring females. The subjects could be historical or legendary and were full of mythical and mystical animals, signs, and numbers.

The number nine, for example, occurs over and over again. During Ragnarok, the god Thor battles with the serpent Jormungand and kills him. Thor steps away as his foe falls, but after taking nine steps, he falls to the ground. He struggles to his feet and takes another nine steps, but again, he falls to the ground. He repeats this a total of nine times as the poison the serpent spat at him during the epic battle inexorably overcomes his system; in the end, the great Thor rises no more.

Another example of this is the story of how two dwarfs, Brokkr and Sindri, fashion an exquisite golden ring for Odin called Draupnir. On every ninth day, Draupnir would produce eight new rings. And as discussed earlier, in his desire to learn the secret of the runes, Odin hung on the tree Yggdrasil for nine days, with a noose around his neck, without food, drink, or comfort, learning one of nine mighty spells each night.

Additionally, in the heyday of Viking pillaging along the coasts of Britain, the marauders would often kidnap young men as slaves and hostages and sail away with them. If the seas became very rough and the ship was in danger, every tenth hostage might be thrown overboard as an appeasing sacrifice to the sea gods.

Another popular saga tells of the Wild Hunt, Furious Host, or Raging Host—the Asgardsreien. It starts on October 31, and spectral horsemen and horsewomen led by Frigga and Odin on Sleipnir, his great eight-legged steed, can be seen racing across the winter sky in company with the Valkyrie and the fallen warriors in training from Valhalla. The sounds are earth-shattering: blaring horns calling the howling hounds, thundering hooves, and raging winds sweeping through the still, cold night.

The peak of the hunt happens on Yuletide, and the furious ride ends on Walpurgis Night on April 30. All the light in the Nine Worlds is extinguished, and the spirits of the newly dead can roam freely to celebrate the final day of winter. It usually has evil connotations as a time when wicked witches consort with devils, but this is one of the many pagan rites that have been cleaned up and adapted to the Christian liturgical calendar as All Soul's Day when the dead are honored.

There is an amazing online source for all the sagas at http://sagadb.org/

Chapter Seven

The Influence of Norse Mythology on Our Lives Today

Norse and Germanic mythology heavily influenced the naming of the days of the week. Sunday is named after the goddess of the sun, Sol. She is pulled around the Earth by her two fine horses. They are chased by the monstrous wolf Skoll who occasionally manages to snap at her ankles, thus producing a solar eclipse. Monday is named after her brother, Mani. His horse-drawn chariot is pursued by the giant wolf Hati. When he almost catches up, there is a lunar eclipse. Tuesday is named after Tyr, the god of war and justice—a difficult portfolio to balance, even then. Wednesday is named after Odin since his name in Old English was Woden. Thursday is named after Thor, the god of thunder. Friday is actually named after the Roman goddess Venus; the Norse connection is that Venus was known as Frigga's star. Frigga was a complex goddess, as she knew the fate of everyone, even after Ragnarok, but she never revealed it. Saturday was named for the planet Saturn. In Roman mythology, Saturn was the god of agriculture. In the Norse pantheon, there isn't a direct correlation as many of the gods and goddesses are associated with fertility, farming, and harvesting, so it is the only name of a day of the week that does not have a particularly Norse connection.

There are many social traditions, especially around Christian religious events, that harken back to Norse mythology: Yule logs, Christmas trees, decorating eggs at Easter time are only a few. Perhaps Santa Claus driving his reindeer through the sky is an echo of the Wild Hunt. There is one story that mentions the tradition of leaving a sack of hay out for Sleipnir during this time. Perhaps this evolved into leaving a plate of cookies and milk or beer for Santa?

Norse Runes

In an overwhelmingly oral tradition, it is perhaps odd that runes receive so much attention. What is a rune? The word means a mystery or a secret, perhaps even a whisper. A rune is a unique symbol representing a letter in the Old Norse alphabet. They were used for writing, as protection, divination or rune casting, and casting spells. There are three variations called futharks, and the oldest dates back to 100 BCE.

The god Odin was so intent on increasing his wisdom that he went to great lengths to gain the knowledge and the power of the runes. He is said to have passed this knowledge on to Freya, who then taught Heimdall, he who guards the Rainbow Bridge. Heimdall taught the runes to the human race.

Apart from representing a single letter, every rune has a group of specific meanings attached to it, and if it falls, or is written reversed or "merkstave," it takes on a negative connotation. Here are a few examples:

M (pronounced mannaz). Overall meaning: man or mankind. It signifies: The Self; the individual or the human race. Your attitude toward others and their attitudes towards you. Friends and enemies, social order. Intelligence, forethought, creativity, skill, ability. Divine structure, intelligence, awareness. Expect to receive some sort of aid or cooperation now. Mannaz Reversed or Merkstave: Depression, mortality, blindness, self-delusion.

Cunning, slyness, manipulation, craftiness, calculation. Expect no help now.

R (pronounced raidho). Overall meaning: wagon or chariot. It signifies: Travel, both in physical terms and those of lifestyle direction. A journey, vacation, relocation, evolution, change of place or setting. Seeing a wider perspective. Seeing the right move for you to make and deciding upon it. Personal rhythm, world rhythm, the dance of life. Raidho Reversed or Merkstave: Crisis, rigidity, stasis, injustice, irrationality. Disruption, dislocation, demotion, delusion, possibly death.

I (pronounced isa). Overall meaning: ice. It signifies: A challenge or frustration. Psychological blocks to thought or activity, including grievances. Standing still, or a time to turn inwards and wait for what is to come, or to seek clarity. This rune reinforces runes around it. Isa Merkstave (Isa cannot be reversed, but may lie in opposition): Ego-mania, dullness, blindness, dissipation. Treachery, illusion, deceit, betrayal, guile, stealth, ambush, plots.

I would like to acknowledge my indebtedness to Ingrid Halvorsen's exceptional website called: Runes, Alphabet of Mystery for the details of the runic alphabet. It can be found at http://sunnyway.com/runes/

Runic symbols were often used as protection on possessions, particularly weapons. Swords, shields, spears, and knives might have a Tiwaz rune engraved on the handle to ensure victory in battle. Runes were also used as decorative motifs on finely wrought containers for precious objects or in wood carvings. The symbols were made up exclusively of straight lines or edges to facilitate carving. In the extremely wealthy households, the drinking vessels, plates, cutlery, and linen might also have runic monograms. Certainly the letters with their particular meanings formed the basis for jewelry design and decoration on works of art, like vases. The use of runes in jewelry design is one of the most beautiful influences of Norse ancestry that prevails today. Modern body painting and tattoo artists owe much of their inspiration to Norse designs.

In terms of literature, Norse mythology was the inspiration for the brilliant fantasy novels *The Hobbit* and *The Lord of the Rings* trilogy by J. R. R. Tolkien and surely also played a part in the *Harry Potter* books by J. K. Rowling. Music too, particularly opera, would be much poorer if Richard Wagner had not submerged himself in his Nordic heritage and produced that thrilling, stupendous, and lushly orchestrated score for *Der Ring des Nibelungen*. Edvard Grieg also composed a fabulous score for his opera about Olaf Tryggvason in 1870.

Norse mythology has also been popularized by Marvel comics, movies and video games, pinball machines in gaming arcades, and of course computer games.

Religious Influences

The influence of Norse mythology is even more visible today in a revival of interest in heathenry, particularly in Scandinavia, Iceland, and the United States of America. This revival has "the aim of forming a faith tradition that is deeply rooted in the ancient past, and yet can speak to the needs and concerns of modern people." (Stephan Grundy, 2015. *God in Flames, God in Fetters: Loki's role in the Northern Religions*). This interest has taken various forms:

Theodism is a religious movement started in 1976 by Garman Lord. He looks for historical accuracy in how he follows the old gods. This is not a matter of simply duplicating rituals but of truly contextualizing old teachings and being able to apply the principles to the modern world. The concept of tribalism and hierarchy are an important part of re-developing this way of living.

Wicca beliefs are more rooted in Celtic than Germanic paganism, but there are similarities mainly in the strong influence of the belief in gods, goddesses, and nature worship. "Wiccan practice involves the manipulation of nature through various rituals in attempts to gain power, prestige, love, or whatever else a Wiccan wants." (Christian Apologetics & Research Ministry. https://carm.org/) There is a committed belief in reincarnation and karma.

Asatru is probably the most important modern pagan religion today. The word means "belief in the gods," and it is expanding steadily in the United Kingdom, France, USA, South Africa, Europe, and particularly in Scandinavia. It was formally founded by a sheep farmer in Iceland called Sveinbjorn Beinteinsson (1924—1993). In 1945, he published a book of Icelandic rhymed poetry. He had a wonderfully sonorous voice and the physical appearance of an ancient Skald. He made regular public appearances reading his poems and reciting the sagas from the Eddas. He has also made many recordings, some of which can be found on the internet today. In 1972, he petitioned the Icelandic government to recognize Asatru as an Icelandic, neopagan, congregation of faith, with the purpose of reviving the pre-Christianization religion of Scandinavia. It was officially recognized as a national religion in 1973 in Iceland—followed shortly by Denmark and Norway.

The present allsherjargooi (priest) is Hilmar Orn Hilmarsson. In 2015, the members opened the very first modern temple to the Norse gods. It is located in Thingvellir National Park, near Reykjavik. Asatru communities are called Kindreds and the meetings are called Blots which means sacrifice. Mead, which is a honeyed wine, beer, or cider, is consecrated to a particular god and, after everyone has taken a drink, the rest is poured out as a libation to that god. One variation of this ritual is a Sumbel which is a toast in three rounds. The first toast is to

Odin, the second toast is to the ancestors and the honorable dead, and the third toast is open to anyone.

The followers are committed to the Nine Noble Virtues: courage, truth, honor, fidelity, discipline, hospitality, industriousness, self-reliance, and perseverance. One should live one's life with due regard to these virtues and, if you succeed, you will go on in the afterlife to "greater fulfillment, pleasure, and challenge." If one lives badly, you will be "separated from your kin and live in dullness and gloom" in your afterlife. The movement is growing steadily and earning more official recognition every day. Recently the U.S. Army and Air Force have added Heathen and Asatru to the religious preferences list their recruits are required to fill to describe their religion.

Asatru Folk Assembly is an offshoot of the initial group in the USA, the Asatru Free Assembly, and was formed by Stephen McNallen in 1994 as a result of dissension about neo-Nazi membership. Membership to the Asatru Free Assembly is based on bloodlines, and although they deny any hint of racism in their practices, they only welcome people of proven Germanic descent. To quote McNallen, "One of the most controversial tenets of Asatru is our insistence that ancestry matters—that there are spiritual and metaphysical implications to heredity, and that we are thus a religion not for all of humanity, but rather one that calls only its own."

The Odin Brotherhood is a version of Asatru, and they call themselves a secret society for men and women who value knowledge, freedom, and power. You can find out more about them online at http://www.odinbrotherhood.com/

Conclusion

Let us return to our main source, the Eddas. One of the many startling issues one has to come to terms with as one delves into Norse mythology is this concept of the cyclical as opposed to the linear. What happens after Ragnarok? We are told that the cycle just begins again, but we are also told that two human beings, Lif and Lifthrasir, survive Ragnarok by hiding in the trunk of the Cosmic Tree. "Thou must know, moreover, that during the conflagration caused by Surtur's fire, a woman named Lif (Life), and a man named Lifthrasir, lie concealed in Hodmimir's forest. They shall feed on morning dew, and their descendants shall soon spread over the whole earth."

The Eddas explain that several gods do survive and that they meet in Idavoll, which is a beautiful, verdant meadow, where Asgard used to be, and they start to build an even more splendid dwelling called Gimli—this time with a roof of gold rather than silver. They mention two other heavens where the dead will rest in peace as well as a dreadful place called Nastrond, which is cold and completely devoid of sunlight where "oath breakers, murderers, and philanderers" will roam. The worst place though is Hvergelmir, where Nidhogg, the dragon who survived Ragnarok, will suck out the blood and "bedevil the bodies of the dead."

Essentially, the world will be a better place, where the gods and the giants live in harmony and humans will not be afflicted by wickedness and misery. So, perhaps each cycle represents a reincarnation, a growth of the soul, gained with difficulty, to be fit to live with god. This idea is not in conflict with Norse mythology, as there are many instances of being re-born, re-made, or transmigrated into another form.

I hope you have enjoyed this foray into the world of Norse mythology, as this is where our story will end—with a final quote from the Eddas:

"If thou hast any further questions to ask, I know not who can answer thee, for I never heard tell of any one who could relate what will happen in the other ages of the world. Make, therefore, the best use thou canst of what has been imparted to thee."

22121143R00024